PART OF A GREATER SOMETHING

Lawrence Doochin

PART OF A GREATER SOMETHING
Discover Your Purpose And Joy In Business And Professional Life

Copyright © 2024 Lawrence Doochin

No part of this book may be reproduced or transmitted in any form or by any means, electronic, mechanical, including photocopying, recording, or by any information storage and retrieval system, without written permission from the author.

ISBN 978-0-9816990-7-3

All rights reserved

PART OF A GREATER SOMETHING

*Discover Your Purpose And Joy
In Business And Professional Life*

Lawrence Doochin

I dedicate this book to my Creator whom I love with all of my heart, mind and soul. I am honored to serve in whatever capacity is most needed.

To my family and close friends, I am extremely grateful for your presence in my life and your unwavering love and support.

CONTENTS

Preface   9

1. What is Your Destination?   13
2. Conditioning   17
3. Joy and the Fruitless Search   25
4. Energetics and Unity   29
5. The Now   35
6. Can We Operate in Business in a Different Way?   39
7. Fear   45
8. Integrity   51
9. Compassion and Gratitude   57
10. We are not the Roles We Play   63
11. The Call   67
12. Discovering Our Gifts   73
13. Money   79
14. Do No Harm   91
15. Control and the Masculine   95

16. Cats in the Cradle	103
17. Unlearning and Humility	109
18. Unbridled Capitalism	115
19. Acceptance	129
20. Forgiveness	135
21. Joy is the Indicator You are on the Right Path	139
22. Faith	145
23. Service	149
Afterword	155

PREFACE

Rejoice! For you are a part of something grand. You just don't yet remember what that something is and what greater purpose it serves for you and for humanity. But you will eventually remember. There is no other way.

When we are part of something and we don't know what it is, it can pose a problem, because being part of something means we're likely supposed to contribute to it in some way. Certainly, we are aware of many things we are a part of. For instance, we may be married and have children, so we have gifts and responsibilities that we're meant to bring to our family. This is a book about seeking and giving more in business and in life, and each reader has likely served in many capacities in their professional lives, each with some type of contribution that was called for. But what if we're a part of something that hasn't yet risen to our awareness in a way that can be beneficial for us?

We often look at things in a very linear and limited way. Our cell phone is obviously a means of communication that lets us call each other, but do we ever ask what additional purpose it serves beyond being a physical device? Why were we prompted to call this person at this time, or why were they prompted to call us? Do we ask why we happened to meet this "random" person at this "random" time? Why did we have a certain experience? Do we ever connect the dots and see how the pieces of the puzzle fit with each other, or are we just going through life with some idea of a destination that we have been told we should achieve? Can we even say what our destination is?

One of the purposes of our lives here, part of a greater something, is to live in tremendous joy. Introspection leads to joy. For when we're aware of what doesn't serve us, we now have a choice to release what is false and what is blocking our innate joy. This is a joy that never leaves us, since it is intrinsic and isn't based on anything that happens to us, or for us. It's not based on whether we receive that raise or promotion, whether the stock market goes up, whether our children get into the best college, or whether our team wins, because we can just as easily be fired, the stock market can go down, or our team can lose. Sounds like a pretty uncertain and unstable way to go through life.

Unfortunately, many do not live in joy, nor do they understand the way to reach that joy. If we are trying to go from North Carolina to California and we go east, it will take us much longer to reach our destination, and we may take many detours. Such is the state of our lives and the world, but it doesn't have to be that way—and it's not meant to be that way.

We each have incredible gifts which are unique to us, and this is the piece of the puzzle that we offer. For we can't be aware of how we fit into the puzzle unless we're aware of the pieces that are around us—this is the greater something which most of us are not yet aware of and which we'll explore. Your gifts are not random. Do not underestimate your capacity to have a powerfully positive impact on those around you and the world; it takes only one small candle to create significant light in a darkened house.

I hope that by the end of the book the greater puzzle will be clearer and you'll be aware of the detours you take that prevent you from experiencing your intrinsic joy.

> WE ARE THEN OPERATING FROM A PLACE OF POWERLESSNESS, WHERE WE'LL ALWAYS FEEL HOPELESS AND AIMLESS, AND BEING HERE WILL LEAD TO GREAT ANXIETY AND DEPRESSION, WHICH IS WHERE MANY OF US ARE THESE DAYS.

01
WHAT IS YOUR DESTINATION?

The first step on a journey is to know where we're going, right? If we don't have a goal or haven't walked the way before, we can get lost. But if we know where we're going, even if the destination seems far away, we can get there.

The problem is that most of us can't accurately describe where we're going with life in general and specifically with our professional lives. Even if we have some idea and can state our goal, we probably can't say *why* we're headed toward this goal with a decent semblance of logic. Although the words and reasons will vary, they will revolve around something like, "Well, this is what my parents did," "This is what is done in this society," or "I am doing this for my kids so they have it better than I've had it." A more telling comment would be one like, "I feel accomplished when I have a lot of money or have a lot of respect from others for what I've done in my career." This is all good stuff, but are we only operating at a surface level? Are we telling ourselves we *should* have a certain belief around our career and this has become our compass?

It is critical to know why we do the things we do and where we are going. If we're operating unconsciously and without awareness of why we make certain choices, we won't float effortlessly on life's currents. Everything will seem like a struggle. We are then operating from a place of powerlessness, where we'll always feel hopeless and aimless, and being here will lead to great anxiety and depression, which is where many of us are these days.

A corollary belief is that everything that happens to us is random. But as we will uncover early in the book, this is false, since we live in an intelligent and structured Universe. Can we see that we are like the gerbil on the spinning wheel, afraid to slow down since we might fall off and fall behind others? Can we see that we're going as fast as we can but we don't understand that we're actually not getting anywhere? This is the ultimate of illusions.

It is critical to know why we do the things we do and where we are going.

MY SUGGESTION OF SUCCESS IS TO RECOGNIZE WHAT IS EPHEMERAL VERSUS WHAT WILL DEFINE YOUR LIFE ON THIS EARTH THAT WILL FAR TRANSCEND YOUR TIME HERE.

02
CONDITIONING

We are a product of conditioning. Our conditioning forms our belief system, and this is how we see and operate within the world. The colored lens we filter our perceptions through is unique for each of us and is constantly changing as we're exposed to new information and new conditioning.

Buddha said that "we are what we think" and that "with our thoughts we make the world." If we don't recognize our conditioning, we are operating unconsciously, similar to how a virus affects the operation of a computer.

Why are we even discussing conditioning in a book about business? Because we are not separate from any aspect of our life. Everything is part of a unified whole, which we will discuss in the next chapter. We can't be a dysfunctional mess in our personal lives and be a healthy mentor or boss in the business world. We can be a star in the business world—many highly dysfunctional people have risen to the top—but this does not align with the greater something we are a part of and seek.

Conditioning can take many forms. In the business world it can be as simple as having a boss in our first job who was condescending and led us to believe that we weren't capable. If we had a parent who treated us the same way, our boss is only deepening the false beliefs we hold about ourselves.

Most of us have been negatively conditioned in childhood to a much greater extent than we realize. Conditioning does not have to be as overt as physical or sexual abuse, for example, though those are certainly types of conditioning. It is often emotional and implicit—as in you are expected to act this way or say this for me to love you. Children are like sponges, but what quality of water are we soaking up?

Maybe you learned from your father that an individual's value comes from working extra long hours, so you don't see workaholism as bad or in any way similar to alcoholism. But they are really just different expressions of the dysfunction around self-judgment and worth. They are extremes—different polarities—and severe conditioning places us in the extremes when it comes to our beliefs and how healthy we operate in our relationships and in life.

Many people realize that they came from abusive childhoods and that they experienced trauma, but they think they can bypass this and not have it affect them. Our parents or caretakers did the best they could with the conditioning that was passed on to them, so we can have compassion on and for them, but it doesn't absolve us from recognizing how this helped to create a belief system in us that is likely not beneficial in many ways. Once we realize this, we have responsibility for not passing on the same conditioning to our children and those we love and to those we interact with on a frequent basis, like those in our business settings. We can't "bypass" false beliefs. We must uncover them and release them, similar to how antivirus software finds the virus and deletes it. For good or bad, we are our own programmers in terms of writing new code.

Burying or suppressing what we want to stay hidden only gives it more power. Only by exposing our false beliefs and conditioning—and seeing how they have affected our behavior, reactions, and relationships—can we see that these are not real. We have created false identities from this conditioning, but we are not our experiences. We are part of a greater something.

Societal conditioning is as detrimental as our childhood conditioning. In the Western world, we are taught that we should achieve the American dream. We should accumulate a lot of money, a big house in a beautiful neighborhood, smart and good-looking kids who go to elite colleges, and of course, a highly respected career. Those of us with advanced degrees and well-established careers take pride in who we are and what we have accomplished.

Our society is based on the concept of manifest destiny, the belief that the economy and our wealth should extend without pause or contraction. Thus we believe similarly as it relates to our personal business careers and trajectory—the gerbil just keeps running on the wheel until it exhausts itself, which is where many people are today.

But expansion without end is a false concept. This is not how the natural world operates. There are periods of hibernation and retraction needed so that new and healthy growth can occur. We are no different. We require periods of stillness and wintering, periods of reflection, ideally each day. In the scheme of time, it has been a very short period that we have not lived in the natural world, which allowed us to be attuned to these rhythms. Now, we are so tied to technology that we have interrupted this natural cycle and all the wisdom that comes from these downtime periods. The smartphone and the constant pinging for our attention has become the gerbil wheel for many.

So far, many of us have not had the time or reflection to see that we are the gerbil and to ask where we are going. We have also not been able to see how much we have been conditioned by a society which tells us who we should be and what we should accomplish to have value.

How do you define success? This is a key destination question. Do you define success as having a long career and rising through the ranks to be top management with a huge salary and stock options? Do you define it as being highly respected in your field or being the founder and CEO of a business that everyone envies? How much wealth do you need to accumulate to consider yourself a success? If you have a goal, do you even know if it's a goal that is worthy (if, as I do, you define "worthy" as one that serves you at the highest levels)?

Why do you define success in the ways you do—where did this belief come from?

My suggestion of success is to recognize what is ephemeral versus what will define your life on this Earth that will far transcend your time here. Are you loving and present in all of your relationships? If you have kids, are you raising them to be emotionally healthy and authentic, spending many hours with them? Are you breaking the cycle of conditioning and allowing them to become who they are meant to be versus who you think they *should* be?

Why do you work? Is it for a paycheck, to be part of a team, because you believe that you have to, so someone will admire your accomplishments, or to be fulfilled in some way? Maybe it is all of these. In whatever you do that brings you an income, does it also bring you joy? Are you being kind to yourself and others? Are you putting something into the world that will create continually expanding ripples of positivity? Are you working for a company or doing a startup that actually has a product that benefits the world?

Socrates said "To know thyself is the beginning of wisdom." Wisdom comes with self-inquiry. It helps us see what we truly want and not what we *think* we want because someone or society told us that is what we *should* want. If we are to find joy, we must pull back the curtain from these false beliefs we have about ourselves. As we move deeper into the book, we will explore more of how we have been conditioned and how we may want to alter our beliefs to better align with who we truly are and why we are here.

WHEN WE STRIVE FOR A GOAL OR DESTINATION THAT IS NEBULOUS AND ONE WE CAN'T DEFINE, IT WILL BE IMPOSSIBLE TO KNOW IF WE HAVE EVER REACHED THIS GOAL. THUS WE WILL LIVE IN A CONSTANT STATE OF ANXIETY.

03
JOY AND THE FRUITLESS SEARCH

The false belief that a vast majority of us hold and that has been reinforced by society and often our parents is that we are somehow incomplete. That we must achieve something, have a certain amount of wealth—that something outside of us will complete us, make us whole, heal us in some way and give us joy. This is why movie stars, pro athletes, and those who have risen to the top of the business world are idolized. We think we want what they have.

We live our lives as *"If only"*—if only I had *this* amount of money; if only I was Vice President of the company; if only I was this weight; if only I could look younger; if only I could find my perfect soul mate (and you know these people who have gone from relationship to relationship). *If only* never arrives because when we reach the first if only, we substitute it with the next if only …. as this is our defense mechanism against looking within to find our contentment and joy. The Dalai Lama said "When you are discontent, you always want more, more, more. Your desire can never be satisfied. But when you practice contentment, you can say to yourself, 'Oh yes—I already have everything that I really need.'"

We are on an endless and fruitless search for an unknown destination. When we strive for a goal or destination that is nebulous and one we can't define, it will be impossible to know if we have ever reached this goal. Thus we will live in a constant state of anxiety.

It is impossible to find answers in something when it is constantly changing. Change is the only constant in the world and in our lives. Look at how your beliefs have evolved over time, especially when you have been presented with information that has allowed you to see things from a different perspective (unless you are one of those people whose beliefs are so rigid that you won't allow any new information to come in, which is a byproduct of severe conditioning). If our beliefs are constantly changing, why would we ever place strong credence in what we believe today?

My point is that our beliefs are formed from our conditioning and are not us. *They are just what we believe.* We can believe that a bunch of money will make us happy, but there are tons of people who have reached this "goal" and found emptiness. Or others, like the billionaires, continue the game to accumulate far more than they could need—they don't want to acknowledge they are spinning endlessly on the gerbil wheel with no destination that makes sense.

What destination makes sense? If we are not our beliefs, who are we?

YOU ARE LITERALLY THE CREATOR OF YOUR REALITY—THE WRITER, THE DIRECTOR, THE PRODUCER, AND THE ACTOR. YOU ARE THE SCULPTOR AS WELL AS THE PIECE OF MARBLE THAT IS BEING SCULPTED.

04
ENERGETICS AND UNITY

If we are to become more self-aware, it is critical that we raise our perspective so that we can see how we fit into a greater whole, a greater something. How do we fit into the Universe? Only a small minority is aware of the interconnectedness and the basis of life that science has revealed over the last 100 years.

Quantum physics has shown us that everything is in vibration and that frequency is the foundation of life. So each of our cells, everything in the natural world and Earth itself, even "inanimate" objects carry their own electromagnetic signature. Nikola Tesla told us that "if you want to find the secrets of the Universe, think in terms of energy, frequency, and vibration."

Only one unified field of energy exists with everything vibrating at different levels. What you see as "solid" is really just an appearance, a lower level of vibrating energy. **There is nothing separate, regardless of appearances.**

Some people feel and trust energetics much more than others. For instance, energetics can be interpreted as just a feeling that something feels right or something feels off, but many people are scared of their feelings and they resort to their thinking mind as a fallback. We have been conditioned, especially men, to see feelings as weak and our logical thinking mind as the only tool we need to use. We trust our logic over our gut feel, but our wisdom resides in our intuition and our heart, as this is how a deeper part of us guides us. As Leonardo da Vinci wisely told us, "Study the science of art. Study the art of science. Develop your senses—especially learn how to see. Realize that everything connects with everything else."

Science has also demonstrated nonlocality, which describes the ability of objects to instantaneously know about each other's state, even when separated by large distances, confirming a unified, one-consciousness reality. Einstein called this "spooky actions at a distance."

Further, everything in the universe from nature to the orbits of the stars to how the atoms in our cells interact is governed by the same mathematical formulas. There is an ordered and intelligent consciousness that underlies all existence, and we are connected to everything.

Most importantly, energy is not a particle or a wave—until it's observed! Think of the implications of this. "Reality" is created by the observer through the very act of watching. It is all one undifferentiated pot of energy, like moldable clay, that can be formed into anything you want by your thoughts (beliefs), as thought is the vehicle of creation in the Universe. You are literally the creator of your reality—the writer, the director, the producer, and the actor. You are the sculptor as well as the piece of marble that is being sculpted.

We are energizing and creating—either consciously or unconsciously. I think everyone would agree that it is better to create consciously. Once we are aware of the power that resides in us, we then have to choose what we want to create for ourselves and for the communities and business settings we are a part of, as the energetics of a business or community, a family, a nation, and all of humanity consists of the collective energetics of each member. What we want to choose to create—or what we have chosen so far—is not always an obvious choice based on a higher perspective and is the subject of much of this book.

There is nothing separate, regardless of appearances.

"THE DISTINCTION BETWEEN THE PAST, PRESENT, AND FUTURE IS ONLY A STUBBORNLY PERSISTENT ILLUSION."

ALBERT EINSTEIN

05
THE NOW

Quantum physicists have also demonstrated that space and time are neither linear nor fixed as they are subject to relative forces in the Universe such as gravity. Have you ever daydreamed where you lose track of where you are and what you're doing? Athletes and highly creative people talk about being "in the zone." This is the present moment or the now. The problem is that most of us don't trust these moments as they happen so infrequently, and thus we don't believe these glimpses are real or that we can access them frequently. Additionally, we feel safe by going with what we know, so these moments scare the logical mind because they appear to be a threat to it.

Have you ever witnessed your thoughts? Have you watched how you have a thought and it leads to another thought and then another thought, on and on—

until you've spiraled down a whole trail of thoughts? Well, if you observe these thoughts, you may first see how meaningless they can sometimes be, but you will definitely notice that these thoughts are always about something in the past or something you think will happen in the future.

They are never in the present moment because that state of being comes from a completely different place within us. Centering yourself in the now has a way of helping you see your problems in a different light and of helping you to make exponentially better decisions. There are many excellent practices to do this such as meditation, sitting in nature, and losing yourself in a creative activity, among many others.

So what are we perceiving when we believe we have a past that is finished and we have a future which we haven't yet experienced? We are experiencing these constructs through a narrow lens of perception that some might call our personality or ego. But again, there's a much greater part of us that we want to access for our decisions.

There's a much greater part of us that we want to access for our decisions.

THE HIGHER WE RAISE OUR PERSPECTIVE BY UTILIZING COMPASSION AND AN OPEN HEART, THE EASIER IT IS FOR US TO SEE WE ARE ALL PART OF ONE HUMANITY, AND THE LESS WE JUDGE OTHERS.

06
CAN WE OPERATE IN BUSINESS IN A DIFFERENT WAY?

The electromagnetic field coming from the heart is 60 times larger than the one coming from the brain. This indicates that this is a powerful energetic field that we are meant to access, but many of us have closed our hearts due to childhood conditioning and trauma that created a fear of being vulnerable and hurt. We're also affected by societal conditioning that has placed far too much emphasis on logical thinking and telling men they are weak if they show their feelings. As previously mentioned, how we operate in our personal life is inseparable from our business or professional life.

When it comes to business, we've been conditioned to be cautious and generally not to trust others. Nothing is sealed with a handshake any more. Many are not true to their word. Thus we have legal documents that cover every contingency, and these documents continue to grow in size and number. One-page NDAs have become four-pagers. We need a sign off on every decision to cover our butt. It's the lawyers who are making all of the money as they create all of these documents and then handle the proliferation of lawsuits as everyone sues each other. You only need to look at the billboards and advertisements for injury attorneys to know the state of our society. Yet, no one questions it. We just keep spinning on the gerbil wheel as if nothing is wrong and fooling ourselves that we're headed to some grand destination, which as discussed no one can actually elucidate. We are all a bunch of emperors running around without clothes but not talking about it.

We are not meant to live in this way. Our heart has a strong electromagnetic field because it's intended for us to live through it. Operating from an open heart doesn't mean that we are pushovers and can't be strong when needed. We can be compassionate in our personal and business settings while being firm and not allowing others to take advantage of us. It is important to note that compassion starts with ourselves. Carl Jung, who was the father of analytical psychology, said that projection was one of the most common phenomena. Thus, when we are not being compassionate to others, we're not being compassionate to ourselves, and this is needed to operate from an open heart.

Living from an open heart allows us to see that we're not separate. It takes us out of tribal mentality and out of an "us versus them" view. The higher we raise our perspective by utilizing compassion and an open heart, the easier it is for us to see we are all part of one humanity, and the less we judge others. We want good to come to others as we want it to come to ourselves and those we love. Contrary to the ego-based thinking of the world, we do not get ahead by hoarding. As we give, we receive, for nothing is separate. As we do good for others, we receive this in turn. This includes abundance of all kinds—love, joy, wealth, and much more.

Change in the world starts with you—literally. This isn't meant to just be some spiritual platitude/generality/cliche that resonates with us on some distant level but that we forget a minute later, as most people do. The Buddha quote earlier in the book—"we are what we think ..."—reminds us that the world we see and operate in is created by *our* thoughts. So when we make a change, everything in the Universe adjusts to that change. One candle in a dark house throws off a lot of light. As we start to release our conditioning and live from an open heart, we will cause incredible ripples all around us.

The great thing about the Universe is that it has endowed us with a system of self-interest. I'm not defining this self-interest as someone grabbing as much power and money as they can. It's self-interest because when we live from an open heart and our true selves, *it makes us feel good.* And this in turn makes us want to do it more.

Living from an open heart allows us to see that we're not separate. It takes us out of tribal mentality and out of an "us versus them" view.

THE PROBLEM WITH FEAR IS THAT IT'S REALLY GOOD AT HIDING ITSELF, SO WE CAN'T UNDERSTAND WHY WE HAVE CERTAIN REACTIONS OR REPEAT THE SAME PATTERNS IN OUR RELATIONSHIPS.

07
FEAR

There is a lot to unpack when it comes to fear. In fact, I wrote a whole book on the subject called *A Book On Fear: Feeling Safe In A Challenging World*.

Fear is not something to be afraid of, but it is something to be aware of because it greatly affects our actions. Many of us work around our fear by medicating it, suppressing it, or denying it. We strategize and create defenses in our relationships to not have to deal with it. All of this also happens in our business relationships and settings. As I mentioned earlier in the book, we are discussing a wide range of topics and conditioning which one might not think was relevant to business or our professional lives. But business, like everything in life, is just a vehicle that is taking us to some destination, and you can't understand how the car is getting you there without discussing the fuel or type of tires, for example. If we want to continue to think of it in car terms, fear is like the restrictor plate on a supercharged race car that prevents it from reaching its full potential.

Fear is an energetic, a belief, and an emotion. We carry fear individually and as a collective. Each of us has individual fears that are different from others, and there are some collective fears that a large majority of us share, like what happens at death.

The problem with fear is that it's really good at hiding itself, so we can't understand why we have certain reactions or repeat the same patterns in our relationships. Some of the more obvious, surface-level fears are ones like dying in a pandemic, losing our job, not having enough money, or not finding a life partner. But many of these surface-level fears are supported by more deeply entrenched fears. For instance, we may have a fear of not finding a life partner because we have a fear we are not lovable. Or our fear over money may be tied to a fear that the Universe is not a supportive and loving place and that everything is random and that we live in a dog-eat-dog world. We may have a fear of failure or someone taking advantage of us or not living up to someone's (perhaps ours, our parents', or our supervisor's) expectations. We are complicated beings when it comes to our emotions, reactions, beliefs, and defenses. Acting without conscious intention and not understanding why we do the things we do keeps us in unconscious dysfunction and leads us away from joy.

Fear is rampant in many companies, both internally felt by employees and externally imposed by management. It is used to scare suppliers into discounts—"You cut prices by 10 percent, or you will lose the business." Those trying to climb the corporate ladder fear not being the best or falling behind and not doing what everyone else is doing. But fear is also imposed by the company on employees, sometimes subtly and sometimes in a very obvious fashion. The belief is that someone will be more productive if they fear losing their job, but I would strongly question this assumption. We are not fear-based beings. This is conditioning that has been imposed upon us. We are attracted to kindness and respect, and if you supervise someone in this way, they'll respond with a much greater and heartfelt commitment to their job. If they're not doing their job, of course they need to be apprised of this and that termination may be the result, but this doesn't have to be communicated through fear.

Fear, as in fear of missing out ("FOMO") and not keeping up with others, is used extensively in marketing to sell products and services. Shouldn't we be selling products on their attributes and in an air of positivity versus scaring someone to buy?

Fear starts from the top down within companies. As we keep coming back to, nothing is separate, so a CEO who lives in fear and dysfunction in his or her personal life is not going to be some amazingly benevolent and helpful mentor and boss within the company. Remember: energetics drives everything. When we give our power to something—when the board of directors has approved this CEO and the employees of the company have agreed to work for the company—we have implicitly agreed to live with how the company is run. Thus, the energetics of the company, and to a certain extent our energetics when we work for the company, will match those of the CEO and board of directors.

It is important to note that fear is usually behind anger. We can, and we should strive to, get to a place in our relationships where we don't speak from uncontrolled anger that spews at someone and demeans them in some way. We can speak from anger but in a way that is respectful of each party. Obviously, many have a long way to go in this regard in business and in their personal lives. We can witness our reactions, especially our anger, and ask what the belief is that's behind it. And then we can trace back from there and ask what the conditioning that created this belief is. In this way we unwind our false beliefs and conditioning, improving ourselves and being a more authentic human being who is contributing positivity to the world.

What you fear, you will bring to you—even if you are not aware of it—as it is our fear programs that run underneath our awareness that are the strongest. Remember, the Universe is agnostic. It will bring you what you energize.

"THERE COMES A TIME WHEN ONE MUST TAKE A POSITION THAT IS NEITHER SAFE NOR POLITIC NOR POPULAR, BUT HE MUST TAKE IT BECAUSE HIS CONSCIENCE TELLS HIM IT IS RIGHT."

MARTIN LUTHER KING, JR.

08
INTEGRITY

Integrity is a good barometer as to the state of a society, and by this measure, we are not doing well. We have had a severe decline in our morality, which is the fabric which holds a civilized society together.

We go from the mild—like when we're on the "do not call" list and we're robocalled for credit cards and car warranties—to the obscene, like the elderly being scammed out of life savings, and even to the horrendous like child prostitution rings. We have cosmetic surgery for every body part, injury lawyers, violent video games, prescription drugs for conditions we didn't know we had until they told us they needed to be fixed, happiness advertised to us in all kinds of products or services we're actually either already happy without or that won't fill the empty void we think they will. We are looking outward when our joy can only be found by looking inward.

We have regressed into a greater tribal, separatist mentality where we see others as people to be judged and hated because they simply believe something different. Can there be any question as to what we're creating and why the state of our society is unraveling with lower integrity paralleling this fast decline? The integrity and morals of our society reflect those who collectively make up that society. Maybe we should all look in the mirror.

Integrity in our business settings is rarely valued. In fact, it is almost the opposite. Many who have accumulated a large amount of wealth and risen to the top in their business career have stepped on others to get there, taking actions which are morally reprehensible and often borderline illegal. They have thrown integrity out the window, but our society often puts these people on a pedestal. Many companies do whatever it takes to increase the bottom line, regardless of the consequences. This can be everything from treating suppliers poorly to making employees work far too many hours to causing great harm to the Earth and to human health and wellbeing by putting products out that should by any sane measure be banned.

The great Indian spiritual teacher Jiddu Krishnamurti said, "It is no measure of health to be well adjusted to a profoundly sick society." One of the purposes of this book is to have you take a pause and to step back and see that you are a cog in a profoundly sick society. We worship money, material possessions, reputation, career accolades, and worse as our gods. Several pretty wise people have told us not to worship false idols, as it doesn't end up so well. Because we are worshipping something false, we are not centered in who we truly are, and we will take actions that are far out of integrity.

Most people do not understand energetics and the laws of the Universe. You reap what you sow. If you live outside of integrity, you try to scam people, or you assist others who are not acting in integrity, there are consequences to your actions.

This will seem very obvious, but it needs to be stated. *Every choice we make has consequences.* Unfortunately, many people today dismiss the obvious. The natural outcome to my statement is that we should think long and hard before we make decisions which might cross the line on integrity. What are the potential consequences for myself, my family, my community, my business, and humanity? Yes, we should expand to think in the broadest of terms because most people are making decisions with their head against the base of the tree, thinking that life is only the hard and stubbled brown surface right in front of them. But if we rise to the top of the forest, we see a much different perspective.

So we think we can rip people off, scam them, lie to them, or cheat them and we can get away with it. And in the short run it may appear that we've gotten away with it because we have someone's money, for example. But these actions will come back like a boomerang because the same will be done to us in some fashion.

We each must take responsibility for ourselves and what we put into the world. This starts with integrity. Honestly, I can't live with myself if I do something that's out of integrity, like taking advantage of someone or creating harm in some way. I wasn't always this way. If someone forgot to charge me for an item, I didn't say anything. But I am grateful for the change in me.

If we get still, if we put our phones or iPads down for extended periods, we can begin to access that part of us which cannot live outside of integrity. It is there. We are just moving so fast on the wheel that we won't stop to listen and feel into who we really are outside of these roles and identities we hold in the world.

Once we start allowing our integrity to slip, it becomes a slippery slope. We begin to justify actions as okay—"This person deserved this," or "This won't hurt him too much." Again, we are really good at fooling ourselves through intellectual reasoning, but energetically we can't fool ourselves. Self-judgment arises when we are not in alignment with our deeper self, but we deny, suppress, and medicate it with stimulants or the accumulation of more toys and trinkets as we spin endlessly on the wheel. We have come up with an infinite number of ways to fool ourselves. All the while, we die a slow death because we are denying who we are and what we truly want.

We can choose to restore our integrity in one moment. We can decide that going forward, every action we take will be in integrity, even if a situation arises where temporarily this appears not to be a beneficial course of action for us. The Universe is a loving container that wants to bless us and it is waiting for us to give it the green light. We can have both great abundance and high integrity at the same time. In fact, *this is the only way we are meant to operate in the world.*

AS WE OPEN TO MORE MALLEABLE BELIEFS, WE REALIZE THAT EVERYTHING IS NOT SO BLACK AND WHITE. LIFE IS KIND OF GRAY, WHICH ALLOWS FOR COMPASSION.

09
COMPASSION AND GRATITUDE

If we are to operate from a position of authority in our business settings, we must come from a compassionate place. Compassion comes from an open heart and allows us to see that we are not separate, that we are all in this together. If we have to reprimand a member of our team, can we place ourselves in their shoes? By doing so, we can impart the info without being condescending. This allows the message to be heard and integrated with the best possible outcome.

In the chapter on conditioning, we talked about the colored lens through which we each view the world. No one holds the same set of beliefs, and everyone acts based on their beliefs which they see as "truth." Further, our beliefs are constantly changing. The problem is that people believe they are seeing absolute truth, but these are actually relative truths, as they depend on the observer (our faces are pressed against different trees in the forest). If we're all seeing from different perspectives, what good does it serve us to defend a belief to the death or criticize another's beliefs?

In his book *The Holographic Universe*, Michael Talbot frequently refers to the work of David Bohm, who was one of the preeminent quantum physicists of the 20th century. Many quantum physicists believe that the Universe is a hologram. In a hologram, each part contains the whole, and this aligns with the spiritual traditions which talk about the whole Universe and God being represented in everything, even a grain of sand.

When we have a set of beliefs, especially if they are fixed and not open to change, we are seeing through our narrow lens, which is just a small slice of the hologram. We mistake this for reality, when reality is the whole hologram and far more encompassing and inclusive than we are seeing—like seeing reality from top of the tree instead of from the trunk.

As we open to more malleable beliefs, we realize that everything is not so black and white. Life is kind of gray, which allows for compassion. When we apply this in our business settings, we see that it might be wiser to operate more as a collective when it comes to decisions. Yes, ultimately the CEO needs to make the call, but this should only be after taking in all viewpoints and being okay with using another's path. We can be much more effective decision makers—actually much better human beings—if we're not so hardened in our beliefs and we can allow new information to lead us on a different path when needed. Universal energy is always flowing and isn't meant to be dammed up or obstructed. This allows for the best course of action to naturally present itself, which can't happen when the energetic and physical head of the organization is hardened in his or her beliefs and has a psychological need to be seen as strong and right because of their dysfunction.

Gratitude aligns with compassion, because when we operate from a place of self-compassion and compassion towards others, we are grateful. Studies have shown that being grateful creates positive changes in the brain and greatly affects our mental and physical health and overall wellbeing, even helping us to see from more of a "we" perspective.

What these studies are confirming is that gratitude is the engine of the Universe. When we are grateful, we are energetically expansive, and more abundance of all kinds will be brought to us. As discussed, thought is where everything originates and what creates our reality. When we want to create something new—maybe we want to manifest the most amazing job that has all of the attributes we want—we need to create and energize this before it can become "reality." We do this by opening our heart and feeling the joy and gratitude of it happening, *as if* it has already happened. Because only the now exists, it actually has already happened when we think of it— there is nothing in the "future." It is similar to planting a seed in the garden and watering it (energizing it), knowing that it will eventually pop its head above the surface (the actual job we're seeking comes across our radar, for example). But if we stop watering it (stop energizing it), it will die.

Gratitude is a choice. Sometimes when we are in the depths of depression and lower energetics, experiencing resentment, bitterness, anger, or fear, for example it can be a hard choice, but it is something we can force ourselves to do, and this will expand our energetics. Certainly, we can be grateful for those who love us, but we can always be grateful that we are alive and can read these words—or even that we can take the next breath. Once we open to gratitude, it is amazing how quickly the Universe will support us to get out of the rut we are in. But we can't see ourselves as a victim in any way, as this is giving our power away.

AS WE GROW IN SELF-AWARENESS, WE BEGIN TO SEE THAT THE UNIVERSE IS ASSISTING US IN INNUMERABLE WAYS. EVERYTHING IS A VEHICLE TO HELP US COME TO A HIGHER AWARENESS OF OUR PURPOSE, OUR GIFTS, AND OUR PATH TO JOY.

10
WE ARE NOT THE ROLES WE PLAY

We are literally made of stardust. Our bodies consist of particles, forged in the nuclear fusion of stars, which have been in existence for billions of years and will continue for billions more.

This should give us a little broader perspective. One of the benefits to rising to a top-of-the-forest perspective is that it not only helps us see the world and others in a new light, but it also especially helps us see ourselves in a completely new way. We begin to ask who we are and where we have come from. We realize that we're not the roles we play and not the identities in which we have invested so much. These are only vehicles for a greater purpose. Then we begin to ask what that greater purpose is, and that is when the fun starts. Pulitzer Prize-winning poet Mary Oliver asks, "Tell me, what is it you plan to do with your one wild and precious life?"

Aristotle was another wise sage who echoed Socrates and told us that "knowing yourself is the beginning of all wisdom." As we grow in self-awareness, we begin to see that the Universe is assisting us in innumerable ways. Everything is a vehicle to help us come to a higher awareness of our purpose, our gifts, and our path to joy. As we pay attention, we laugh at and are grateful for the ways in which the Universe is speaking to us—a book that happened to be left on the subway, an offhand comment by a coworker, an animal that repeatedly appears to us, or a recurring dream, for example. We can't have partial randomness in the Universe. That is like saying someone is partially pregnant. Either everything is random, or it's all happening within some ordered consciousness with a purpose.

As we come to know that nothing is random, we feel greatly relieved as we know at the core of our being that we are loved and supported. We may not yet have even a partial understanding of why we are here and what our greater purpose is, but we now trust in something greater than us, even if we don't have an idea what this means. This trust is the panacea for our fear and anxiety, allowing us to live more in the moment and experience our innate joy.

Pulitzer Prize-winning poet Mary Oliver asks, "Tell me, what is it you plan to do with your one wild and precious life?"

THE CALL WILL LEAD US TO GREATER AWARENESS. WHETHER WE UTILIZE THIS TO GROW OR GO THE OTHER WAY AND DOUBLE DOWN ON DENIAL IS UP TO EACH OF US.

II
THE CALL

Renowned mythologist Joseph Campbell wrote extensively on a universal archetype that is a prompt or call from the Universe to start on a hero's journey towards a greater awareness of ourselves and our purpose. Sometimes we are forced into change, like when we lose our job or the stock market crashes, and other times it's just a feeling that we're supposed to be doing something different, something that will fulfill us to a much greater extent. Usually a sudden change like losing our job, for example, comes *because* we have not been paying attention to and acting on the call.

Those of us who have had careers in the business world have gotten pretty good at playing the game, myself among them. My experience in the business world has encompassed many areas. I have worked for a large family printing business, worked for and called on numerous Fortune 100 companies, and cofounded several startups. Most of us know how to make and accumulate money. We are experts at sales or marketing, IT, private equity, logistics, operations management, and the like. We can do it well, and it's what we've been accustomed to. A majority of us don't think twice about it because we've been told—or rather, conditioned to believe—that this is what we're supposed to do. We go to college and often to graduate school, we get our first job, and then we start rising through the ranks and accumulating wealth. And then before we know it, we retire—and a big hole is there that we try to fill with golf or hobbies—and we literally wait for death. If we're lucky, our health holds up and we're not put in a nursing home.

Is this not how it goes for a large majority of people? We do these things because everyone else does them, but we never question them. And because we think it isn't real, or it's silly, or we're afraid of what people will think of us if we quit our successful corporate career or law or medical practice, we never pay attention to The Call. Campbell has a point to make about ignoring The Call:

"If a person has had the sense of 'the Call' – the feeling that there's an adventure for him — and if he doesn't follow that but remains in the society because it's safe and secure, then life dries up. And then he comes to a condition in late middle age: he's gotten to the top of the ladder and found that it's against the wrong wall."

And further, he says, *"The hero's journey has been compared to a birth: it starts with being warm and snug in a safe place; then comes a signal, growing more insistent, that it is time to leave. To stay beyond your time is to putrefy. Without the blood & tearing and pain, there is no new life."*

Putrefy is a pretty harsh word, but it is accurate. As I have arrived at 60 years of age and I ponder and feel into what the last third of my life will look like, I look around and see a lot of sad people without a purpose, and I know I want something different. For I have honored The Call and gone through the blood and tearing pain, and I know that depression comes from not aligning with our gifts in a way that helps humanity. My heart is asking to be of service.

The Call can happen for the collective, and it can define a generation and change the course of history, like the protests against the Vietnam War. When the collective is called to do it differently, a large number of individuals is affected, since individuals make up the collective. The Call is happening now for each of us individually and as a collective. This was the case with the Covid era; large numbers of individuals across the world were forced to examine their fears, their career choices, their blanket giving away of authority to those in power, and much more. As difficult and horrific as Covid was, many came out of that period with a greater sense of what they wanted going forward, like not traveling for business to the extent they had previously done. Many had important realizations about their relationships—and thus about themselves—when they were forced to be in isolation with family members. This led to a beautiful renewal of relationships as well as the breaking apart of others. The Call will lead us to greater awareness. Whether we utilize this to grow or go the other way and double down on denial is up to each of us.

"To stay beyond your time is to putrefy. Without the blood & tearing and pain, there is no new life."

THE UNIVERSE TEACHES US THROUGH CONTRAST. WE SEE WHO WE ARE AND WHAT WE WANT BY SEEING WHO WE AREN'T AND WHAT WE DON'T WANT.

12
DISCOVERING OUR GIFTS

As we discussed, in the business world we usually know what our gifts are, since they're used in that arena. For instance, I am a masterful salesperson. Not only am I very detail oriented and a great project manager, but I also know how to read a situation and person and move the person from the initial contact to a sale, where that's possible. I interact with the person I'm trying to sell to as I would a good friend and energetically they feel this, a dynamic which makes them comfortable with me and instills a desire in them to want to do business with me. I am not manipulating them—I am just being myself—but "myself" has changed a lot over the last 30 years as I have taken The Call and released a lot of personal and societal conditioning, leading to a much greater self-awareness. So I really see the person across from me as a part of one humanity and universal collective, even though they rarely will consciously see that in themselves.

We usually go through a set of experiences before we receive The Call so that we can recognize it and it can show us contrast. The Universe teaches us through contrast. We see who we are and what we want by seeing who we aren't and what we don't want. As mentioned, I worked for several Fortune 100 companies in my twenties before I came back to a mid-sized family printing business. The Call led me to leave my family's business in my late thirties for two years, during which time I wrote a book and supposedly "found myself." But The Call often has many stages—if we don't stop its natural flow—and these stages lead us to more realizations, the release of more conditioning, and greater levels of joy and contentment.

When I left the family business, it was necessary for me to energetically disengage from my birth family, but at the same time I was also running from something and fooling myself. How can these both be possible? The Universe holds many paradoxes. When I went back to the family business two years later because I needed to financially, this wasn't a mistake or a failure of any kind. *We learn from our mistakes, and this is how the Universe operates*; this is how we know to do it differently the next time. So there really are no mistakes if we get the lesson that will lead us to greater self-awareness.

The Call has led me to found or participate in three startups. Two of these failed, and one has been successful. The first two failed because the energetics of the founder, who founded both companies, was not there in terms of abundance. He didn't believe at a core level that he deserved to do well, and there was no way that these companies could work as long as he owned the majority of stock. I certainly did not understand this when I invested. We used to get to the altar on outside funding, only to be rejected, and I eventually came to see these ventures as hot air balloons, but ones with the ropes still attached, so they could only rise so far. When I realized that these ventures were not going to work, I immediately cut my losses and said I wasn't going to invest any further funds.

Was investing in these companies a mistake? By the view of those who fund startups and the investment community in general, it would be considered a loss and thus a mistake, or at least an option that one wouldn't take if the choice could be made again. But if we rise to a view from the top of the forest, it wasn't a mistake. When I invested in this first company, I did it because I had a strong feeling this was something I was supposed to do. Yes, I had a number of conversations about the product and its potential, but I went with the feeling that intuitively guided me, since I had learned enough to trust The Call. I had learned enough to trust that I was being supported and that this action was a path to my highest good, even when I couldn't understand the big picture or where these current choices might lead me in the future.

I believe one of the reasons I was guided to invest in these two startups was to learn a hard lesson about energetics so that I would be successful in other areas of my life, including my latest startup. By the way, I believe that The Call for the founder of the two failed startups was the ideation and invention of some amazing products. But we have to understand where our gifts lie and what our blocks to energetics are. He wasn't willing to go down the path of self-reflection to understand that these companies could never be commercially successful because of his blocks. Taking an unbiased and unemotional appraisal of our gifts and areas where we don't have strengths might mean that we invent the product but sell the company to someone who can make it commercially successful. It might mean we hire a management team and are no longer involved in the day-to-day operations. In no way does this mean we are a failure, although many think we are if we take actions like this.

In order to drive home the point, I continue to emphasize that we live in a loving Universe. As part of that, the Universe is taking us on a long journey towards self-awareness and the release of what is false. It is similar to peeling the layers of an onion. Some move through this process quickly, and some may take longer, but it doesn't really matter. What matters is what *you choose*, because the Universe is here to support your choices. It's important to understand this as we process what we may deem as "negative" experiences. How many times have we seen an experience as negative but have subsequently come to see it as a blessing? This helps us to see from a higher perspective, which has the potential benefit of helping us realize how our gifts might be applied in greater service.

We also need to expand our definition of how we are gifted. As indicated, most of us know that we're a great surgeon or coder, but what have we been gifted with as a human being? Are we a great listener? Do we automatically have empathy with someone else? What is it that makes our heart sing and beat faster when we think about it or do it? What gives us pain when we think about it? All of these are pointers.

EVERYTHING HAS A NATURAL FLOW AND RATE OF GROWTH AS WELL AS A HEALTHY AND NECESSARY CONTRACTION—
FROM NATURE, TO OUR RELATIONSHIPS, TO OUR SELF-AWARENESS, OUR WEALTH, AND MORE.

12
MONEY

I think most people from the business and professional world have at one time or another questioned the relentless pursuit of wealth accumulation. At least, I hope they have. But our conditioning has us quickly dismiss this questioning, even when we can't give a satisfactory answer to the question (or we just fool ourselves and justify it with some nonsensical logic).

Like everything in the Universe, money is energy. But like everything in the Universe, it is meant to flow and to be used for the benefit of the collective. It is not meant to be hoarded.

Have you considered that we're placing our faith in something that's not even tangible? What is money anyways? It's a medium of exchange for something of value, but in our digital age, money exists in its essence as no more than a series of computer entries. Can we eat these or even exchange them for food? It's not like we haven't experienced times throughout history during wars and financial panics when money wasn't accepted or lost its value. We are also placing a lot of faith in technology, which consistent and catastrophic technological crashes have shown us to be misguided faith. As we increasingly rely on technology for our everyday lives, are we not opening ourselves up to a lot of risk?

Governments create money out of thin air with the click of a computer command. This is against natural law, since new energy cannot be created—it can only transform and move from one state to another. Everything has to return to its mean. As mentioned earlier in the book, natural cycles do not expand without end. Since there are consequences to every action—a reaction to every action—we have to pay the consequences to our choice to operate outside of natural law. This means that when an inevitable contraction occurs, it'll be much worse. This is why we have financial, housing, and other types of bubbles that have to crash—with devastating consequences to individuals who are caught up in a highly dysfunctional system that others control.

Although this is present in all industries, I have seen this firsthand in the packaging industry. A company comes along that is funded by private equity or venture capital and tries to grow very quickly, which is contrary to natural law. Everything has a natural flow and rate of growth as well as a healthy and necessary contraction—from nature, to our relationships, to our self-awareness, our wealth, and more.

When a business tries to grow quickly, there are only two main ways this can happen. In the packaging industry these companies have either rapidly acquired other companies in the industry, and/or they submit below-market pricing to acquire new business. These companies don't have a secret sauce that allows them to price business at 30% below their competition, nor are there large economies of scale and reduced raw material pricing from vendors, since diminishing returns have already been reached. So there is no economic rationale for what they're doing other than to grow quickly, but because they're running business at unsustainable long-term rates, they require outside funding to prop this scenario up. As well, the companies that are purchasing competitors at a rapid rate require outside funding to make these acquisitions happen, and this scenario is not economically justifiable either—if they are purchasing companies that have actual long-term value with equipment, personnel, and accounts, they're having to pay above-market premiums to entice these companies to sell, and their return will be many years out.

Again, these types of business transactions are distortions that can only be achieved by outside resources. A strong energetic foundation is built over many years through excellent quality and service and long-term customer relationships, which is how my family's business—and many in the industry—were built. The end result of these distortions? There have been several. I have seen many of these large packaging companies, which for years had below-market pricing to maintain their business, either go under or be sold to other packaging companies at deep discounts. Because what value are accounts worth if they can't be retained unless it is with below economically feasible pricing? Many of these companies have lost large chunks of business during the supply chain issues of the last few years as their service level became intolerable for the large consumer product goods companies, regardless of their pricing. These companies were running on the edge to start with, as their funders, the venture capitalist and private equity firms, had stripped them of any excess fat ... so that they could look the best and be sold to the next buyer.

This is really a game of musical chairs where you don't want to be the one left without the chair. It's a type of Ponzi scheme, its only purpose being to make more money. This idolizing of money has been bad for the world, bad for so many individuals affected by this system, bad for the earth, and yes, bad for those who operate and facilitate this game that's far removed from their purposes and callings on this earth. This system is collapsing because it's unsustainable and in violation of natural law.

The macro patterns mentioned above trickle down to the micro level and are applicable in our personal lives around money. Again, money is energy and is meant to flow. We are meant to pick the ripe fruit and then seed other gardens with it. When we pick the fruit and prune the tree, it is much stronger going forward. This is how the Universe works. We receive in order to bless others. As we bless others, in turn we receive more than we had before—the tree grows stronger and produces more beautiful fruit.

Unfortunately, most wealthy people don't operate from this space. While there are exceptions, the increasingly larger amounts of wealth we have insulate us from the realities of how others have to live on a daily basis. This situation leads us to make decisions which we'd never make if we didn't have excess wealth and which are not in alignment with our deeper selves and our source of true joy. Studies have shown that emotional well-being and happiness begin to diminish after a certain point of income—$105k for those in North America.

Even when we give to charities, we're usually giving to ones that are top-heavy with management and administrative fees—meaning a smaller percentage makes it down to the actual cause we are giving to—and ones that align with what we want to see happen in particular arenas, like the furthering of some special interest championed by a group we care about. Basically, we're giving to a cause which reinforces separation and tribalism over unity. One thing I hope we could all agree on that would reinforce unity is that everyone on the planet should have food, shelter, clothing, and access to basic health care. Certainly, there is more than enough wealth for this to happen multiple times over. Again, for most of us who have grown up in the US in middle-class to wealthy families, we are shielded from how hard people have it across the world and even here in the US. I'm not speaking to anything that most of us don't already know, but we've chosen to ignore the elephant in the room. As long as it's a big room, the elephant is in the corner, and someone else has to clean up the poop, we don't have to deal with it or acknowledge it.

I get a good laugh when people say that unbridled capitalism is good. *Too much of anything is usually detrimental.* Unbridled capitalism has led to a huge wealth disparity. Maybe you are okay with that—I am not. Our rights don't come from the government or some system—capitalism, socialism, fascism, democracy, or something else—but are endowed by God or whatever you want to call the creator of the Universe. This means that we each have the right to basic necessities and to live in joy. If we have been privileged to be born into wealth, or we have been afforded opportunities to create a lot of wealth, *this was not random.* We have the responsibility and the privilege to help others not so fortunate.

In addition to the wealth disparity, unbridled capitalism has created many other ills. We continue to rape and pillage the earth, which we're not meant to conquer. Such a separation mentality can only lead to hubris. Instead, we must live in a symbiotic host and caretaker relationship with our planet. As discussed earlier in the book, we can see the state of a society that happens when money becomes a god—a breakdown of morals, a blurring of integrity, large increase in addictions and perverse acts like pedophilia, blatant dishonesty, worship of those who are not the best examples—the list goes on and on.

When we don't understand that money is energy and we don't allow financial abundance to flow as intended, the energy becomes stuck, and it weighs us down in many ways, affecting our mental and physical health. We actually crave simplicity. We can live in simplicity and have great abundance passing through us. These are not mutually exclusive. When our goal is to accumulate as much wealth as we can, we greatly complicate our lives because we're dealing with multiple attorneys and financial advisors or we have numerous trusts and tax shelters, for example. We spend our time dealing with the minutiae instead of *staying in the now, trusting the Universe to provide what we need, and experiencing the great joy in life and in blessing others.* If we're worried about where the financial markets are going or what will happen to the economy and how it'll affect our wealth, or if we're constantly adjusting our trusts to take advantage of new laws and how much we will pass on to our children, we are living in the future. Actually, we aren't even living, since we're trying to figure out what will happen at our death. We might as well be stars in a zombie movie.

While there are of course many exceptions, a large majority of wealthy and ultra-wealthy have allowed money to become their god and their pursuit of it to be primary in their lives. Some have earned and increased their wealth by engaging in unethical or morally reprehensible practices. This can even be categorized as founding or being involved with companies which have products or services that are not beneficial for humanity and the world. So again, integrity is easily blurred, especially if everyone else is doing it, which society seems to actually condone.

The relentless pursuit of wealth affects everything around a person, especially their relationships and time with family. What many don't realize is that being present for your family and raising emotionally healthy children, if you have children, is one of the greatest things you can do for the world. It has much more far-reaching significance than how much wealth you accumulate and what impact you make in your professional life. Finally, it's evident that few wealthy people understand how the Universe works and how wealth is energy that is meant to flow, not be hoarded. If people/society/the collective/the world understood this reality, no one would be ultra-wealthy. They would have blessed others less fortunate as soon as their wealth increased to levels beyond anything they could need to be very comfortable in their daily lives. They would trust the Universe to meet their needs and always give more. We would see an individual's wealth move up and down, for as they receive, they give, and as they give, they receive more.

Buddha taught us that our attachments lead to suffering. We think the more money we have—the more we have of anything—the happier we should be. But this is the ego mind and the logical left brain thinking. It's not how reality works. What actually happens is that the more wealth we pursue in order to acquire and hoard, the less joyful it makes us, and the more we erroneously ramp up the pursuit in order to fill that absence of true joy. Simplicity leads to greater joy. This is a path that many have walked the talk. You don't have to live off-grid with nothing but the clothes on your back, but you do have to ask *What are my priorities? Where does my joy come from? How do I want to spend my time? What am I chasing?*

WHEN MONEY IS INVESTED AND COMPANIES ARE PURCHASED WITH THE SOLE CONSIDERATION BEING THE QUICKEST AND LARGEST RETURN ON INVESTMENT, WE ARE DOING HARM.

14
DO NO HARM

There is a reason that all of the world's religions and spiritual traditions, even the Hippocratic oath, have the philosophy of "Do no harm" as a main principle. As shown below, it's stated in different ways, but they all come back to the same golden rule.

Buddhism	Hurt not others with that which pains yourself.
Christianity	Do unto others as you would have them do unto you.
Judaism	What you yourself hate, do to no man.
Hinduism	Treat others as you would yourself be treated.
Islam	Do unto all men as you would wish to have done unto you.
Native American	Live in harmony, for we are all related.

A lot of wise people have told us we should operate in this way. "Do no harm" must be pretty important.

Doing no harm is both explicit and implicit. Certainly, we can see the explicit ways in which this sacred principle is being trampled upon. Everyone is attacking each other with significant verbal harm across social media and other platforms. As discussed, many in business rise to the top by stepping on others and doing harm. We are greatly harming the earth, and we only have one of those to live on.

But doing harm can be implicit and hidden in many ways. When we allow unbridled capitalism, such as when we tell people that their happiness can be found in some toy or trinket that's shipped halfway across the world, or in cosmetic surgery for who knows what body part, or that we're victims and we should always look to sue because that's our right and we've been wronged, we are doing harm. When a large retailer forces a supplier for whom the retailer is a large part of their business to sell at super low margins, and the retailer chooses to move to another supplier over a penny, the first company is put at risk of going out of business, and we are doing harm. When money is invested and companies are purchased with the sole consideration being the quickest and largest return on investment, we are doing harm. When the performance of CEOs is based on a quarterly financial result instead of longer-term growth and especially how the company is benefitting its other shareholders—employees, suppliers, the earth, all of humanity—we are doing harm. I could continue ad infinitum.

Unless we live in a cave, we each participate in this system, which means we have explicit and implicit responsibility to some extent—usually to a great extent. When we ignore the poop from the elephant in the room, we are implicitly doing harm. As much as some of us would like to separate ourselves from our actions and the fact that we are part of one collective and live as one humanity on one planet spinning in the Universe, we can't. So we might as well begin to recognize this and take actions which align with our highest truths. We could all learn a lot from someone like St. Francis, who picked up worms from the wagon paths so they wouldn't be crushed. He was doing his part to do no harm to benefit even the smallest of life.

WHEN WE WANT TO BIRTH SOMETHING NEW LIKE A STARTUP OR A CREATIVE ENDEAVOR, WE MUST BALANCE THE MASCULINE ASPECTS OF ACTION AND THE FEMININE ASPECTS OF RECEIVING INTUITION AND GUIDANCE FROM THE UNIVERSE.

15
CONTROL AND THE MASCULINE

The business world and our systems of power are heavily male-dominated. This is not by chance. We have endured several thousand years of patriarchy that has denied and suppressed the inherent feminine aspects we all carry—thus denying the gifts of creativity, intuition, and compassion—and created the world we see today. Even when a woman is in power, like the CEO of a corporation, she often tries to show she is strong and can do the job as well as a man, which in her eyes means she must be tough and can't come from her heart.

Business has devolved to unbridled capitalism and a deficit of integrity because it reflects an imbalance tilted towards the masculine—misuse of power and accumulation of wealth to benefit individuals and special interest groups at the expense of others, humanity, and the earth. When we are tilted too far towards masculine attributes, we have to be the best, the smartest, the best-looking, or the wealthiest, and we have to be in control, regardless of what it takes to get there. In addition to what is mentioned above, we are missing the balancing feminine attributes of equality, acceptance, fairness, justice, empathy, and especially being heart-centered. Regardless of our gender, we all have these attributes. But they've been repressed as we've been conditioned by society and other sources to believe that these characteristics are weak and that we won't make it in the world if we exhibit them. When individually we are not in balance, this distortion feeds into the collective with imbalanced power structures and systems.

It is also not by accident that women have these attributes and the ability to give birth. For the Universe is constantly in a state of creation. This is not only what mystics have told us but also what science has proven. When we want to birth something new like a startup or a creative endeavor, we must balance the masculine aspects of action and the feminine aspects of receiving intuition and guidance from the Universe. This will help us find the best path to success along with the desire to make something which will be of benefit to the founder of the venture, their family, and hopefully for the world as well. All businesses, even the largest corporations operating today, started out as an idea to fill a need and to create something of value. Few founders likely thought, "I'll do this and make a lot of money." But we have moved away from these more altruistic founding principles as these businesses have grown to be behemoths, operating under a system where making the most money possible is often the only goal—a strong tilt towards the masculine. And because of this conditioning, a large majority of startups today are not founded on altruistic principles. They're founded with the goal of making a lot of money and are operated with the idea that the company only needs to get to a certain point in revenue or users before it is an attractive buyout candidate.

The private equity firms have the same goal, which is a separatist mentality that benefits only the management and shareholders in these firms. The sole goal of selling a business for a large multiple over the original purchase price only leads to the destruction of healthy businesses as they lay off employees and make other cuts so that their companies will show a large profit over the succeeding few years, enabling firms to sell them to the next buyer. Collateral damage like the devastation of long-term and loyal employees and their families and the energetic and physical devastation of a long-established business, because you can only make so many cuts in a body before it bleeds to death—well that's just part of how capitalism works, right? This is the same bury-our-head-in-the-sand and don't-look-at-the-elephant-in-the-room denial of the reality that there is immense wealth in the world and that still, people are starving. It's not my problem because it's not at my doorstep, right? We are at the pinnacle of imbalance. In this case the destination of "make as much money as possible" and "just take care of ourselves and our families, regardless of the cost," is pretty obvious, but is anyone stopping to ask why this is the destination?

It is hard for us to see these imbalances when we have had literally thousands of years of patriarchy encoded in our genetics and in societal life. A few matriarchies still exist today, but they are found in small indigenous tribes. There were numerous matriarchies existing across the world thousands of years ago as described by historians at that time. However, by the time of the Roman Empire and the birth of Christianity, the males had been in charge for a while. In fact, at the Council of Nicaea in 325 AD, only males gathered to determine what would be included in the official book of Christianity. Many of the writings found in Egypt in 1945, known as the Dead Sea Scrolls, included writings like the Gospel of Thomas. They were excluded by the church fathers at Nicaea because they spoke to a more feminine balance of equality and to the fact that we each can connect with the divine without going through an intermediary.

In addition, these writings spoke of the concepts of sin and penance in a completely different light, offering a much different version of God than the judgmental and punishing one, which traced back to the writers of the Old Testament—highly likely male. Those deciding what would be included in the Bible could not let these "heretical" writings, many of which were thought to be recorded and written during the life of Christ, *before* the actual accepted gospels which are generally accepted as written well after his death, see the light of day if control was the goal. But in reality, Jesus showed us how to operate with a balance of the masculine and feminine. He used anger and power only when necessary—like his throwing the moneychangers out of the temple—while staying in the feminine aspect of great compassion. What he showed us is that love is not weak and is to be strived for in every situation.

So we have been conditioned to believe in and operate from an imbalanced masculine side for a long time. And we pay the consequences in many ways. This imbalance plays out in all aspects of life—from our relationships, in which men are afraid to cry and be vulnerable, to whether a business is beneficial or detrimental to humanity, to how we relate to and treat the earth. If we bring in more of the feminine, we will see a natural return to healthier relationships, integrity in our business dealings, and releasing of the need to control others. It will mean an honoring of all aspects of ourselves—especially offering ourselves compassion instead of self-judgment, a reduction in blaming others whom we don't agree with (for judgment of others is a projection of self-judgment), and the ability to access a deeper and wiser part of ourselves.

It's not my problem because it's not at my doorstep, right?

THERE IS NOTHING TO ACHIEVE. THERE IS NOTHING TO PROVE.

16
CATS IN THE CRADLE

Most people know the iconic song "Cat's In The Cradle" by Harry Chapin.

Its lyrics always make me sad, as they're so reflective of how many live their lives.

> *My child arrived just the other day*
> *He came to the world in the usual way*
> *But there were planes to catch, and bills to pay*
> *He learned to walk while I was away*
> *And he was talking 'fore I knew it, and as he grew*
> *He'd say, "I'm gonna be like you, Dad."*
> *"You know I'm gonna be like you."*

So the child ends up growing up to be like his dad, and they never connect. When the dad is retired and wants to connect, the son is too busy. And I always think about how the son is likely passing the same pattern on to his kids.

Life is about determining what our priorities are. For most of recorded history, extended families lived together, and the grandparents raised the children while the parents worked. Now many are chasing a career path that causes them to relocate every few years, and children may see their grandparents twice a year. Extended families also historically took care of the elderly. We have gone from the responsibility and honor of keeping the family unit intact by caring for those who took care of us when we were young to a proliferation of nursing homes where in essence, these beloved family members have been placed to die. No wonder they're depressed and go downhill quickly.

My wife and I built our house over 32 years ago, and although we recently sold it, it was always a place where our kids could come back to and feel grounded. Remember energetics. Our home had 32 years of love and laughter and tears, some anger, and some dysfunction, but it was always a container for our family. Certainly, it is not possible for some families to live in the same house as long as we did, but we all need grounding in the familiar, as it anchors us and gives us courage to navigate life, which has become somewhat difficult for many people.

I am not criticizing the choices that any one individual or family must make, like placing elderly parents in a nursing home. When you have a broken system, the choices are hard. But as with much of this book, I am reminding us of how broken the system has become, which most are enabling and not questioning. How do we fix a broken system? Since we're each a part of it, individually we must disengage from the system and make different choices. We must create new systems, which start with small choices—we do our best, knowing that if everyone makes small choices, collectively we beget big changes. It's actually comforting to know that all we have to do is our part.

As discussed, our choices have consequences that ripple out to many shores. Are we properly evaluating the choices we make based on criteria that takes others into account, especially our children and parents—and even all of humanity? Are we holding ourselves accountable for the choices we make involving our career, or are we, based on conditioning, just living in denial and shooting for some imaginary goal that we think will fulfill us? If we are in denial, we are turning away from a higher path, and there will be pain and sadness involved with this ignorance of our inner truth, even if we don't consciously recognize this. In order to suppress the pain and sadness of not listening to what we truly need and want, we medicate it with any number of stimulants, addictions, or diversions, but we can't really suppress it. It will find a way to keep coming back for us until we pay attention.

We can learn a lot from indigenous peoples because they understood there was truly nothing to achieve. Life itself, just being alive, is a blessing and is where our joy lies. Our joy also lies in being part of a community where the members truly support each other. It lies in being of service to others and the world in some way. It lies in connecting with the greater part of ourselves.

Indigenous peoples also understood the concept of balance. They didn't separate work and play, since their way of living was all in a flow of what was required and what they wanted to do. So maybe one member of the tribe was the bow maker, and he did this role, since it was essential to the tribe. But maybe he also participated in the hunt. He was both a specialist and a generalist, unlike our roles today which have become highly specialized. And he also had an equal amount of time for community and play. Everyone in the tribe did.

There is nothing to achieve. There is nothing to prove. What a novel concept that's so foreign to how we operate in the Western world. We are searching for something outside of ourselves, and we will never find it—because it is illusory.

ALL THINGS ARE POSSIBLE IN THE UNIVERSE—WE ARE ONLY LIMITED BY OUR BELIEFS OF WHAT IS NOT POSSIBLE.

17
UNLEARNING AND HUMILITY

Because of our conditioning, we have to *unlearn* many things in order to make decisions from a clear space that are for the highest good of ourselves and others. We believe we understand how life works, but when we start to unlearn, we're surprised that we don't understand much at all. Socrates told us, "The only true wisdom is in knowing you know nothing."

That is a bold statement. What it tells us is that we're operating in a sphere of reality and belief that is illusory. There is a different type of intelligence or wisdom that doesn't come from the world—like from a book or what an expert or leader tells us. It really doesn't come from anything outside of us. We're all living to a certain extent in a delusion. Some are drowning in it, evidenced by the state of the world. The fortunate ones are those who recognize they're in a delusion.

Shouldn't we all be seeking to see the delusion and find our fountain of true wisdom?

The famous Chinese philosopher Lao Tzu confirmed the distinction between knowledge—education and learning that comes to us from the world—and wisdom when he said, "To attain knowledge, add things every day. To attain wisdom, remove things every day." This advice runs so counter to how the world thinks, since we're encouraged by society to constantly improve ourselves and learn more. There are all kinds of hacks and programs to help us reach greater mental aptitude and focus. But are we feeding a part of ourselves that is taking us away from true wisdom?

As discussed earlier in the book, we're taught to accumulate more, to be smarter, to be better looking through cosmetic surgery—taught that we shouldn't be satisfied with who we are and what we have. Because we're looking for the next thing to add or do in order to, we hope, reach this mythical apex of contentment and self-acceptance, we miss the very obvious point that taking away things makes life simpler. If we take the wheel out of the gerbil cage for intermittent periods, we will eventually learn not to run as fast when the wheel is in the cage. This is why it's important to have still periods or downtime each day and extended still periods like retreats as often as responsibilities permit. I promise we won't become vegetables if we allow our minds to quiet and be still. If anything, we'll rediscover a deeper part of ourselves, which will give us joy and the ability to make choices which are exponentially more effective.

It's really hard for some people to admit when they've been wrong and that maybe they don't have enough information to judge others or make a proper decision in a situation. Acknowledging the futility of judging others is not weakness. Rather, it's strength that allows us to move into humility—which is important, because we no longer have an agenda. We are then open to receiving from the Universe the best course of action. Jesus told us we needed to be like little children to enter the Kingdom of Heaven. Have you ever seen a young child full of hubris and arrogance?

I was recently speaking with our younger son, who was going through some angst around finding a new job. He had been working for four years at one company and felt like it was time to move on, so he finished off his job as an independent contractor for the last few months. He was down on himself because he felt like at times he hadn't given his all to the job, so energetics were not complete when he left. It's important that when we leave one job, we have given it our best effort and are leaving because we're being pulled to another calling. But even when this isn't the case, the Universe wants only our highest good and for us to learn from our "mistake" so that we do it differently the next time. Self-judgment needs to be released.

He was also comparing himself to others and their skill levels. Comparison is a tool of the thinking mind that is based on judgment. In order to feel better about our situations, we compare ourselves to others who are less wealthy, less intelligent, or worse looking, for example. But in a Universe that reflects unity, differences are only an appearance. As we become more self-aware, we stop the comparison.

As I told him, staying in guilt, self-pity, and comparison achieves nothing but closes us off to the next opportunity because we're not radiating the energetics needed to create what we want. All things are possible in the Universe—we are only *limited by our beliefs of what is not possible*. I told him to envision what he wanted in the ideal job and energize that, knowing he can have whatever he wants. Although he has to apply and

UNLEARNING AND HUMILITY

contact people and follow up, the Universe does the heavy lifting. Even if the job he wants doesn't yet exist, his continued energizing of it will create it—someone will have an idea and create a new position that, incredibly, matches up to what he's energizing.

My point is that he has to unlearn all of the conditioning that he's believed about how the Universe works, what's possible, how much joy and abundance he is entitled to, and how he doesn't have to worry so much and try to figure things out or control situations, among other lessons. When we come to these realizations, we naturally fall into humility, since we realize we don't understand much at all and that life is one great mystery. We can just sit back, trust in the benevolence of the Universe, walk through the doors that are opened for us and ride the wave. The more we live this reality, the greater life will open for us.

WE NEVER TRACE
BACK TO WHY WE TAKE
CERTAIN ACTIONS AND
THE CONSEQUENCES
OF THOSE ACTIONS.
THIS IS OUR PERSONAL
RESPONSIBILITY AS
MEMBERS OF ONE
HUMANITY.

18
UNBRIDLED CAPITALISM

We briefly mentioned unbridled capitalism in an earlier chapter, and it's helpful for us to look at this concept in more depth. When a horse has a bridle, it keeps the horse under some type of control and moving towards a destination that makes sense—the horse isn't going from one side of the track to the other but rather is headed toward a finish line, a goal that everyone agrees on.

Nothing in the Universe is "good" or "bad"—it's how it's used that's "good" or "bad," and each of us individually, and all of us collectively, must determine whether it's serving the highest good. So, as with all things, capitalism can be a great engine of change for beneficial or for destructive purposes.

It is obvious that in many cases capitalism has gotten out of control. There are many more products and services than we could ever need. Remember simplicity—after some basic necessities, the less we have, the more joyful we actually are. Many of these products, manufactured in sweatshops, are shipped halfway across the world at an enormous financial and environmental cost. We have large-scale mono crop farms which destroy the soil and are only maintained with high levels of fertilizers and pesticides when regenerative farms have shown us a way that works with nature, instead of against it. A large percentage of the Western world, and sadly, a large percentage of children under five years of age, are on prescription medicine. Do we not realize that anxiety and depression are tied to unbridled capitalism, especially our never-ending pursuit of what can never give us contentment?

Maybe our metaphorical gerbil is running endlessly on its wheel because of great anxiety from being caged, similar to how other animals and humans react—with addictive and compulsive behaviors—when under a constant level of stress. Are we not running endlessly on the wheel of life and pursuit of some unknown goal because of our own anxiety about being so far removed from how we are meant to live in harmony with others and the Earth? Are we living in a cage of our own making that's been created by accepting what others and society tell us we should be doing?

Do we dismiss the fact that so many young children are growing up in a world where they are surrounded by non-native, man-made electromagnetic fields (EMFs) from technology and that this fact is causing a large part of their behavioral issues, most of which were rare when kids didn't have smartphones and tablets and were outside all day in the sun with their hands in the dirt? There's a tremendous amount of research and peer-reviewed studies on the health dangers of man-made EMFs and hundreds of highly credible scientists, researchers, and medical professionals having spoken out at the risk of their careers. The FCC approved 5G, which operates at a completely different bandwidth from 4G, without conducting any research studies. This is unbridled capitalism at its worst—when we subject our children to our inability to regulate ourselves and protect them. They are innocent, but our choices are not. Lots of elephant poop here.

We are tearing down perfectly sound and livable houses to build mega mansions or building two, tall skinny houses on a postage-stamp-sized piece of land to maximize profit, often on busy roads where kids can't even play. Somehow, we have bought into the concept that we don't need any trees or nature and that the closer to the city we are, the better. Where I grew up and lived most of my adult life, which was in the suburbs of a major city, development continued to encroach on the wild places. Somehow it is seen as progress when condos have balconies that directly overlook the interstate, or we are so fortunate because all of these restaurants, dry cleaners, drugstores are within a mile, and we have multiple cell towers near us and we get five bars on our devices. Unbridled capitalism has made us forget that we evolved and lived in nature, which has for eons had highly beneficial native EMFs—because everything is energetics—and it's made us believe that we don't need nature anymore, that technology is the answer to everything. I wasn't even living in the densely populated part of the city, but when I left the suburbs for good and moved to living on the land, I looked back and wondered how in the world did I ever survive that constant level of high stress.

My father died a few years back, and my stepmother sold their house in a wealthy enclave of the city I grew up in. The house is on several acres, but the land was designated as a 100-year floodplain, which meant that the house couldn't be completely torn down to build another. The house was extremely well constructed with a well-laid-out floor plan and plenty of room for a family with 6,400 square feet. Instead of just remodeling the house, the new owners stripped it down to its studs, and it was that way for several years. There was likely twice the money put into the house than what it sold for, which was significant. *Having an extreme excess of money often insulates us from living in some type of reality where we step back and say, "Do I really need to do this?"*

The world has become an industrialized and homogenized factory farm where every supermarket, from the northernmost to the southernmost countries, carries fresh produce year-round that has been shipped across the world. The newest cargo ships are behemoths that emit as much pollution as *50 million cars*, and there are thousands of cargo ships.

Do we need to be driving vehicles that cost $100k when we can drive one that costs $35k and is very comfortable and reliable? Do we need to build a 10k-square-foot house for just two people and our dogs? Do we need five TVs in our house or to redecorate every five years? Do we need the latest phone when ours work properly—and when we understand that those same phones are made by sweatshops using rare minerals and other components of which there is not an inexhaustible supply?

Many studies have shown that bee colony collapse is tied to pesticide use. American homeowners use *ten times* more pesticides domestically than the quantity that's used in agriculture. Why should we care? Because bees pollinate a huge amount of our food. We would care if our floorboards were rotting in our house and then just collapsed one day. Do we need to have perfectly manicured lawns, using poisons to achieve it, when it's obvious that's not how nature works and the chemicals are doing a significant amount of damage—and we're doing it just to make ourselves look good to our neighbors? We never trace back to *why* we take certain actions and the consequences of those actions. This is our personal responsibility as members of one humanity.

There's a big difference between what we need and what we want. (I have seen actual marketing that says you don't need it but you want it). Unbridled capitalism says, "Get whatever you want; you deserve it, and you don't have to care about what it took to make it or get it to you. Just keep buying stuff—it will make you happy!" And of course we need to get it overnight, or even better yet, tonight from 8 to 10pm!

The fact is that we're just complicating our lives and *choosing* to be busy and distract ourselves with diversions and stuff so that we won't be still and connect to that deeper part of ourselves. We need to turn inward for what we are seeking. This doesn't mean that we should live like monks and can't enjoy the things of the world. But again, with all of our choices, we need to be honest as to our motivations and we need to explore the consequences of our choices. Some choices are much more benign than others. If I want to eat some chocolate after dinner because I have a craving, but I know that it'll likely disrupt my sleep, then I'm really just affecting myself (although my wife might disagree if I'm tossing and turning!). But for a majority of our decisions, we are creating a wide-ranging ripple that has consequences for other people, our communities, and the planet—so my suggestion is to consider the ripples before you just say I want it.

I have a large amount of faith in the intrinsic goodness of people, and I know that aside from a few bad players, most people would make different decisions if they connect with their heart and fully examine their motives and the potential consequences of their decisions. But I also know that societal conditioning and messaging that we should always do what is in our self-interest is well entrenched. And we are taught to rely on our logical mind instead of accessing our heart wisdom. Thus, this separatist and linear mind perspective is how we've ended up with the world we see today. Individually, it's our societal obligation—and our family obligation to stop lineages of dysfunction and abuse— to "know thyself" and to break free from societal and personal conditioning.

I'm not excluding myself from my admonitions of our current situation, as I participate in it as well. It's kind of hard not to. So I have compassion for myself and everyone living in this broken system. But I recognize I don't want to participate in it any more than needed, and I take steps where possible not to contribute to it. My seven-year-old phone works well. I'm able to only wear one pair of pants and shoes at a time, so I don't need a lot of new clothes. I'm learning to grow food, not only because it's a good idea, but because it puts me more in touch with what is real. Because this consumer- and marketing-driven unbridled capitalistic society is not real if we view reality as embodying and honoring who we really are and what we truly want, even if we keep fooling ourselves otherwise.

As mentioned above, with acknowledgment comes responsibility and the requirement to choose as well as the understanding that *there are no small parts or insignificant contributions*. Do you choose to continue to stay in denial and do the same things you've been doing, or do you choose to do your part to make a difference? This is a really important choice that has far-reaching ramifications related to who you are and your place in the Universe.

Jesus said, "For I was hungry and you gave me food. I was thirsty and you gave me drink. I was a stranger and you welcomed me. I was naked and you clothed me. I was sick and you visited me. I was in prison and you came to me. " Jesus was speaking from a universal aspect and referring to the divinity that is within each of us. When we do an act of service for another, we are doing it for Jesus and all divine beings, which includes ourselves. There is only the One and we must choose what kinds of seeds we are sowing. Before we give to our special interest groups or organizations—which are only reinforcing separation—can we not acknowledge our unity and humanity and start with the most basic needs of food and shelter as Jesus was trying to help us understand? Can we not?

Again, we need to take a step back and understand how we have come to this place. This allows us to see the insanity of it all. For instance, It is hypocritical and arrogant to judge another for the circumstances they've been born into. No one wants to take handouts from the government or organizations unless they've been conditioned and incentivized to do this. When a welfare system is set up to maximize benefits if a single mom remains unmarried, would anyone in their right mind think that the end result would not be an epidemic of single moms raising multiple children by different fathers?

It's not up to some external source like the government to mandate or put a bridle on capitalism. As we discussed in our chapter on integrity, we each have to be the ones who make the change and who hold the line. Each of us must choose how we want to employ our wealth to make us at peace with ourselves and to do our part in the world. We must lead by example, and others will follow. It doesn't take many of us to act individually to shift the collective, since research has shown it's only 25%.

Capitalism is not "bad." It is just a vehicle, like everything else in the Universe. The vehicle of capitalism can be beneficial for the world if utilized in a very different way from our current model. Let's call this holistic capitalism, since it factors in all stakeholders, including the earth. This model of capitalism would be one where the only corporations who exist are the ones offering products and services that benefit humanity and the earth in some way. Employees of these corporations would be paid a salary much more equitable to that of upper management, and everyone would receive a share of the profits. Thus, each employee would feel valued and would feel joy at contributing to something that is of immense benefit to humanity. Holistic capitalism would not exclude the reality of some individuals having more resources than others, as some have the innate gift to properly handle and distribute these resources. But these individuals would also understand that they have a great responsibility to be channels through which financial and other resources could come in and flow back out in order to benefit the whole. Some might call my proposal socialism, but what many people do not understand is that throughout time, under the guise of being benevolent leaders, all systems of governance have been co-opted by those in power who are acting purely from self-interest. Holistic capitalism is not only possible; it is essential to replace the current model, which is headed over the cliff as it is unsustainable. When something is so far from its natural center and in violation of the laws and the framework in which it was created, like a rubber band which has been stretched too far, it will either break or snap back to its center.

How have we ended up where unbridled capitalism is taking us over the cliff? We have given our power away through our choices. The politicians are only too happy to take the power we give them. The corporations are only too happy to sell us more stuff. Don't expect them to be good citizens. I have worked for and extensively called on and dealt with many corporations, from the largest to the smallest. What I've seen with the public companies is that the shareholder model and emphasis on short-term profit puts even well-intended management teams under a bridle that takes them in the wrong direction. If you're going to lose your job because you don't produce certain results, you kind of pay attention to this and take actions that assure job security.

I've mentioned only a few of the many ways that unbridled capitalism has impacted our world. What I recommend is that we each open our eyes and truly start to look around at how the relentless drive for wealth accumulation and power has negatively impacted so many areas of our life. Most don't yet see how sick the system is. From the outside, everything looks fairly normal, but the warning signs are there. It's like a tree in the forest that looks perfectly healthy but one day just falls over because it was rotting inside. However, the warning signs were present as it had lost a few major limbs in recent years. In many ways, that's similar to what's happening to the current system. Adverse circumstances don't personally have to be the case for any of us if we move our attention from the outer to the inner and listen to our heart, shed our conditioning, and make decisions from this centered place.

WHEN WE FIGHT AGAINST OURSELVES, OTHERS, AND THE WORLD, BASICALLY NOT ACCEPTING THE REALITY OF THE SITUATION, WE ARE REINFORCING A FALSE BELIEF IN SEPARATION AND DUALITY.

19
ACCEPTANCE

We must accept ourselves as we are *while* striving to improve ourselves. We must accept the world and its destructive unbridled capitalism, staying out of denial, *while* recognizing that it needs to change for ourselves, our children and grandchildren, and future generations. Because as we've established, what we are doing is not sustainable.

If the above statements sound paradoxical, they are. This is how the Universe works. Remember that science has shown us there is only one field of unified energy, so there is only *the appearance* of separation. When we fight against ourselves, others, and the world, basically not accepting the reality of the situation, we are reinforcing a false belief in separation and duality. Not being accepting of ourselves at the core of our being and not being accepting of our unique place in the Universe is what causes us to look outside ourselves for our self-worth, and as we've learned, this leads to a whole host of not-so-good stuff for us individually and for the world.

Accepting where the world is and how dysfunctional our systems are, especially in business, allows us to approach our situation from a place of reality so that we can change it. As we become more self-aware and open our hearts, there is no way we won't be angry and sad at times about the state of the world. But accepting and acknowledging where we are allows us to stay removed from the blame game that's so prevalent in our present world. We must understand the difference between judgment and discernment. Judgment tells us that a certain person is taking actions that are "bad" *and* that the person is "bad" or "evil" because of that. Discernment acknowledges the actions as detrimental but sees that we're all part of one whole and that this person is not "bad" but just unaware of how their actions or words are affecting others and the world. "Bad" and "evil" are in quotations here since they're relative terms that will have different meanings based on our particular perceptions and belief systems.

When we work to know ourselves and peel back the many layers of beliefs and conditioning, we become more accepting of ourselves and of others, since again, judgment is a projection of self-judgment. Accepting our conditions without judgment allows us to operate from a grounded and non-emotional place—then we can know the actions we must take or the words we must say to others to do our part to change the world. This set of steps will be quite different for each of us, since some of us may feel the need to write about it, others the need to be in street protests about it, others to have conversations with their friends and families, and others to pray on it—or a combo of all types of different things. Hopefully, many of you will want to found startups or create positive organizational change within your business after reading this book. And what we are led to do may change over time—we just need to open our hearts, set our intentions, and be flexible to follow the paths we are shown.

As we move through this work of self-awareness and the processing of emotions such as anger, sadness, and fear, it is critical that we have compassion for ourselves. Self-compassion softens everything we're going through because it dissolves the self-judgment that's at the core for almost everyone on the planet, especially those of us in the Western world who have undergone societal conditioning that tells us we're not good enough as is. And the incredible outcome of giving ourselves the gift of compassion is that we will automatically have much greater compassion for others, which is really the catalyst for everyone getting together to correct the mess we've put ourselves in.

We just need to open our hearts, set our intentions, and be flexible to follow the paths we are shown.

WHEN WE WON'T FORGIVE SOMEONE, WE ARE PUNISHING OURSELVES AND GIVING THEM THE KEY TO OUR JAIL CELL.

20
FORGIVENESS

There is a great misperception that forgiveness is weak and that we have to be the stereotypical macho man (or woman) to make it through the world and achieve our goals. Actually, the opposite is true.

Believing that hardening ourselves to the world is the only way to navigate it stems directly from the belief that we are separate. If we were separate, then this approach would make sense, since we'd be truly alone and would need to take care of ourselves. Many of us have the perception, however "true" or not, that we can't let anybody take advantage of us, which many believe is the case if they forgive others who have in some way wronged them.

But by not forgiving, we are giving our power away to the other person, since there is an energetic tie not allowing us to make the clearest of decisions—because we still have an agenda—and not allowing us to live free of that other person's dysfunction. Most people think that by not forgiving, they hold the power over that person by somehow punishing them, but in reality, when we won't forgive someone, we are punishing ourselves and giving them the key to our jail cell.

We can—and must—apply these understandings to our professional and business lives because there is no separation within the whole of our lives. How happy and effective we are at relationships in our personal lives and how much of our dysfunction and false beliefs we have released are directly correlated to how effective we will be in our professional or business lives. As we discussed earlier, we can operate a business through fear, non-compassion and non-forgiveness, and it may appear this strategy is effective, but in doing so we're not operating at the true level of doing something good for ourselves, our businesses, our employees, and the world.

Certainly, in the business world, if we have employees, we have to walk the line between expecting a person to do their job and operating from forgiveness. It doesn't really work to say, "You're not doing your job, but I forgive you and give you unlimited chances to get it right." But our professional lives, just like our personal lives, provide huge numbers of opportunities for forgiveness, because forgiveness is one of the primary vehicles through which we grow and become more self-aware. So it may be that our employee is having a difficult day or period in their life and has been rude back to us. We can forgive them and discuss this behavior with them while not abusing our position of authority.

As mentioned, life is not black and white—and it isn't meant to be. Having to see something from another's perspective and maybe even see it from a different perspective from the one we had five years before brings us more into a space of forgiveness and compassion and helps us to sort out what we truly want in our lives. We want to separate our professional lives from our personal lives because that is what we have been conditioned to do. After all, many of us are just waiting for the weekend or our next vacation., But if we step back and stay in the now, we can see the gifts that our professional lives are bringing us. These are gifts far above our compensation or what advancements we make in our career.

TRUE JOY IS THERE ALL THE TIME, BUT IT GETS COVERED UP BY OUR DYSFUNCTIONAL BELIEFS LIKE SELF-JUDGMENT, OVERATTACHMENT TO THINGS OF THE WORLD, CREATING OUR IDENTITY IN WHAT IS FALSE, GUILT, SHAME, OR FEAR, FOR EXAMPLE.

21
JOY IS THE INDICATOR YOU ARE ON THE RIGHT PATH

Not to sound trite, but joy is joyful. It is how we are meant to live life. This is what the Universe wants for us, and it's sad that so few people actually live in true joy.

True joy is inner joy, not the joy that comes from watching your sports team win, getting a raise, or seeing the stock market go up. Some believe that joy can even come from acting like a victim—the false belief being that pity will bring joy. Looking to something outside of you for your joy is transitory and built on a foundation of shifting sand—you will be depressed because the stock market goes down or your team loses. True joy is there all the time, but it gets covered up by our dysfunctional beliefs like self-judgment, overattachment to things of the world, creating our identity in what is false, guilt, shame, or fear, for example.

We must distinguish joy that is temporary and comes from our thinking mind and what is core within us. As mentioned, true or core joy comes from something other than our possessions, relationships, and experiences, and it will feel very different from these. True joy can be nourished in many ways. We can feel it by doing something for someone else, just because they need it. Maybe they don't even know we did it. How counterintuitive does this sound to the world's thinking that we "lose" when we give something away? We actually gain, because there is no separation, so in some way we are giving back to ourselves. And giving actually reinforces our belief that we *have it to give*, bringing us more abundance. This is Universal law 101.

We can also uncover true joy by allowing our artistic gifts to come out—like by just immersing ourselves in painting or making an incredible meal that will feed those we love. It could come out by just allowing ourselves to be a child and be silly. It could come out by being grateful for the smallest blessings in our life and understanding that being present to this is what is real. Maybe it's just sitting against a large tree in the forest and allowing ourselves to feel the wonder of creation. We way overcomplicate life when it's meant to be simple and joyful.

Once we connect with that real joy, we will want to connect again as soon as possible, because it *feels really good*. Our deep conditioning doesn't make it easy, since the whole world is pushing toys and trinkets, experiences, and "shoulds" and "have tos" as the path to joy. We need to remember the feeling of this true joy and ask the Universe for help in accessing it as often as possible. As we energize this joy muscle and decondition ourselves, our true joy will automatically begin to randomly spring up on its own.

The more we experience real joy, the more we can use that feeling as a pointer to get back to it when we're not present in it. Our body's memory of it will lead us back. As we practice this, as we remember who we really are, we can use this joy to help us make decisions. What feels good? What makes our heart sing? If a certain choice does, then the path to go down reveals itself to us. The process is simple, since we trust the Universe to have shown us our highest good—and we only have to follow the inner joy compass. The thinking ego mind does not need to be involved in the decision. It will likely need to be involved in the logistics of how this choice gets implemented, but that is *after* the choice is made. And joy can be a pointer for the smallest of decisions to the largest.

Understanding and feeling true joy is critical in our businesses and professional lives. True joy is a guide reminding us that we are on the right path that is in alignment with what the Universe wants for us as our highest good. True joy helps us to discover our unique gifts that we have been given so we can be of service, which can look many ways. When we are of service and we use our gifts to help others, the planet, and the whole, we then feel true joy to an even greater extent. We are then given more opportunities to use our gifts, bringing us even more joy. What a beautiful endless circle of joy and healing that we are participating in.

When we are of service and we use our gifts to help others, the planet, and the whole, we then feel true joy to an even greater extent.

BUT IF WE ARE PAYING ATTENTION AND WILLING TO NOT RESIST, CHANGE CAN COME EASILY, AND WE CAN SEE IT FROM A HIGHER PERSPECTIVE AS BENEFICIAL.

22
FAITH

Faith is just the trust that something greater than us has our back and wants only the highest good for us. It really doesn't matter if it takes expression through a religion or spiritual belief system. Faith is the innate knowing that you are here for a reason and that you are greatly supported.

If we aren't operating in faith, we will live in fear, and we will try to control life. But doing so doesn't have very good results. Not only is it exhausting, but look at how often we run into obstacles and blocked doors. When we have faith, we know things will work out. Knowing things will work out allows us to have patience and use all parts of ourselves—like our hearts, our feelings, and our minds—to see the highest choice that the Universe has for us. It's as if we're riding on a magic carpet down the river of life, above the rapids and rocks, and being taken to the destinations our higher self has chosen to arrive at. It's this easy if we have faith and allow it.

Faith is inherent, but it is uncovered and remembered by gifts from the Universe. We can look back at our careers and relationships and see how the Universe guided us. We didn't get into a certain college, but maybe we ended up at another and met our spouse. We were laid off from our first job and we took another job in a completely different career field where our gifts could really shine. Or maybe we started a company which aligns with how we want to help the world.

There is a lot of change going on right now, which many perceive as negative since they fear change. But change is the only constant, and it's intended to be beneficial. The change can come forcibly if we haven't paid attention to signs that the Universe is giving us—maybe we are fired or our spouse leaves us. The Universe is always showing us where our false beliefs lie—and the false beliefs of those with whom we interact— and what we're doing that's not serving our highest good, like giving our power away to individuals, groups, or authorities, for example, or denying the need for self-healing and the release of our conditioning.

But if we are paying attention and willing to not resist, change can come easily, and we can see it from a higher perspective as beneficial. We don't have to wait years to look back and see that we fought and resisted all of this change, causing a lot of angst and trauma. We can understand and accept it now, flowing with it. Accepting the change, even when we don't fully understand where it's leading us—and maybe facing fear over this—strengthens our faith to a great extent. Each time our faith is strengthened, we can more fully embrace the next round of change. This is when the Universe can really work with us to be positive agents of change in the world, which as we know the world so badly needs.

> "HAPPINESS COMES WHEN YOUR WORK AND WORDS ARE OF BENEFIT TO YOURSELF AND OTHERS."
>
> —BUDDHA

23
SERVICE

As the book highlighted from the start in the preface, *you are part of a greater something*. This something is partly a mystery, but what I can assure you is that it is incredible and wants only to support you. There are no accidents in the Universe. You are here for a specific reason, and you have unique gifts to employ. Employing these gifts will bring you great joy and will serve humanity in some way.

Many of you reading this book come from the business world, as do I. What few of us realize is that we are in the business world to play our part in a higher calling. Let's call this *The Committee To Do Good In The World* (yes, I know that sounds a little corny!)

Business has gotten a bad rap—but justifiably so. It's a very powerful vehicle of change, but who is driving? Each of us needs to take the wheel. We need to raise our perspective to see how we've been led to this point and what purpose this journey has had for us. In doing so, we know how we need to operate our businesses or employ our wealth going forward.

We look at history to try and extrapolate a future. Just like when we evaluate a chart for a stock, when we assess ourselves and see where we've come from, we can see where we're going. This is because we can see the trend line—giving us insight into why certain events occurred for us to build experience or skills in a particular area. Just as we analyze companies on the decisions they make like when we say, "This was a really good detour they made when they went into this product line," or "Their decision to go overseas was a bad one for these reasons"—we do the same with ourselves. With great compassion. We don't usually apply compassion to a business whose stock plummeted because its leaders made a bad decision, but it is critical to apply compassion to ourselves as we analyze where we have been. Again, there are really no mistakes when we understand that everyone is making "mistakes"—for how else can the Universe teach us the path and choices that are right for us? So, mistakes are just learning opportunities to grow to your next level of awareness.

Now with this new perspective we can begin to dial in our specific gifts and what we want to do with them that will be of benefit to the world—our part in the greater something. But we first have a choice to make. Martin Luther King, Jr. told us that "Every man must decide whether he will walk in the light of creative altruism or in the darkness of destructive selfishness."

I used to be completely aligned with how the world, and the business world, in particular currently operates. Like most, I was going through the motions and doing what I believed I was supposed to do. It wasn't so much a surface belief, because I wouldn't have been able to adequately express it if asked, but it was just deep conditioning (from society and an entrepreneurial Jewish family) that I would never have thought to question. But when it is our time to see a greater truth and experience, the Universe will prompt us. As we've discussed, many will ignore the prompts, and eventually the Universe will have to wake them up with the equivalent of a redwood tree falling on their head. But I feel blessed that for the most part, I have not ignored the prompts. And this understanding and surrender really goes to the heart of feeling joy.

As I began to understand and feel the joy that is inherent in creation instead of looking outside of myself to things of the world, I was drawn to this joy. The Universe sets us up in a system that is very much in our self-interest, because when we rediscover ourselves and the true world around us, this awareness is unlike anything we have experienced before. This doesn't mean we don't still operate in and enjoy the things of the world, but it does mean that we're not attached to these things as our identity or primary reality, since as quantum physics has shown us, we exist in many realities.

As I continue down this path, I have increasingly released that which does not serve me, which has led to even greater levels of joy. And I have become more cognizant of the unique gifts I have that I want to employ in service to humanity, which again, in doing so, will bring me great joy. *The joy of service is what is built into our DNA.*

We are meant to live in true communities, both physical and energetic. This is also part of our DNA. As we align with our gifts and purpose, we will find others who are in a similar alignment. In physics this phenomenon is called resonance.

What I wish for each of you is to find your true joy. My wish for you, and for humanity, is that you become more aware of your existing gifts and discover new ones that can be utilized to be a piece of the puzzle of which we are all a part. For you are needed—and obviously quite badly, judging by the appearance of the world. Let us rejoice as we all fulfill our parts in a greater something.

STOP AND BREATHE, LET GO OF ALL OF WHAT YOU BELIEVE TO BE YOUR PROBLEMS, AND SEE WHAT IS RIGHT IN FRONT OF YOU THAT YOU HAVE BEEN MISSING.

AFTERWORD

It is not what we accomplish in life that matters. It is how much joy we have in doing it and what ripples this commitment to following our hearts creates for others and the world. Are we living life to the fullest? Are we utilizing our unique gifts to do amazing things that make us feel good about our place in the world and how we are contributing to it?

Life is not meant to be complicated. The Universe intends for us to slow down and see the beauty all around us. Stop and breathe, let go of all of what you believe to be your problems, and see what is right in front of you that you have been missing. Appreciate and honor all life, from the smallest insect to your fellow humans. "In the beginning was the Word, and the Word was with God, and the Word was God." We are one creation, and everything around us points to this remembrance, even our language. Uni-verse—one verse (word), one creation.

How do we get started on this grand journey? It starts with the simple desire for something different for ourselves. This intention sets us on the path, and then we only need to walk through the doors that the Universe opens for us. There is great comfort as we begin this journey, for we can take a big exhale and realize that we don't have to be running on the wheel any longer. *We don't want to be running on the wheel any longer.*

We don't have to be in a cage with bars created by our own and society's conditioning. *We have choice.* And with choice, we have power, the power to make our lives incredible and the power to help others see their inherent power and their ability to make their own lives incredible. With choice, we also have responsibility. *To whom much is given, much is asked.*

But this is not a burden. Fulfilling our roles in helping the world is a joy, an honor, and a blessing. We have been given the world to mold in whatever way we want. We can be grateful while also understanding that the ramifications of honoring our gifts and fulfilling our roles goes far beyond anything we can comprehend. How everything interconnects and where all of the ripples extend is the mystery of the Universe. Many

AFTERWORD

people can't handle the mystery part because they want to control the outcome. But nothing in life, even our next breath, is guaranteed, and when we can finally surrender to this truth, it allows the current of life to carry us to the most amazing destinations. Ironically, only in giving up control and trusting in the Universe do we find wisdom and what we've always been looking for, even though we probably didn't know that's what we were looking for in the first place!

So, I'm wishing you good travels. Be easy on yourself and give yourself—and others—a lot of grace. The ride will become much easier.

Larry

For more information on who I am and my background, please visit my website at **lawrencedoochin.com**.

If you benefitted from reading this book, I would greatly appreciate your leaving an online written review.

Thank you!

www.ingramcontent.com/pod-product-compliance
Lightning Source LLC
Chambersburg PA
CBHW031420290426
44110CB00011B/467